MOZART

First paperback printing 2013
First published in North America in 2007 by the
National Geographic Society
1145 17th Street N.W.
Washington, D.C. 20036-4688

Copyright © 2007 Marshall Editions
A Marshall Edition
Conceived, edited, and designed by Marshall Editions
The Old Brewery, 6 Blundell Street, London N7 9BH, U.K.

Paperback ISBN: 978-1-4263-1451-3
Hardcover ISBN: 978-1-4263-0002-8
Library ISBN: 978-1-4263-0003-5

Design and editorial: Tall Tree Ltd
Picture research: Caroline Wood
Consultant: Professor Julian Rushton

For Marshall Editions:
Publisher: Richard Green
Commissioning editor: Claudia Martin
Art direction: Ivo Marloh
Picture manager: Veneta Bullen
Production: Anna Pauletti

For the National Geographic Society:
Art director: Bea Jackson
Project editor: Priyanka Lamichhane

One of the world's largest nonprofit scientific and educational organizations, the National Geographic Society was founded in 1888 "for the increase and diffusion of geographic knowledge." Fulfilling this mission, the Society educates and inspires millions every day through its magazines, books, television programs, videos, maps and atlases, research grants, the National Geographic Bee, teacher workshops, and innovative classroom materials. The Society is supported through membership dues, charitable gifts, and income from the sale of its educational products. This support is vital to National Geographic's mission to increase global understanding and promote conservation of our planet through exploration, research, and education.

For more information, please call 1-800-NGS LINE (647-5463) or write to the following address:

NATIONAL GEOGRAPHIC SOCIETY
1145 17th Street N.W.
Washington, D.C. 20036-4688 U.S.A.

Visit the Society's Web site at www.nationalgeographic.com.

Previous page: The manuscript copy of *Eine Kleine Nachtmusik* ("A Little Night Music"), in Mozart's handwriting. He wrote it in 1787 and it remains one of his best-known compositions.
Opposite: A portrait of Mozart at age 33 carved in boxwood by Leonard Posch (1750–1831).

Printed in China
21/QED/3

MOZART

THE BOY WHO CHANGED THE WORLD WITH HIS MUSIC

MARCUS WEEKS

NATIONAL GEOGRAPHIC

WASHINGTON, D.C.

CONTENTS

A MUSICAL PRODIGY

1

CONCERT MASTER

2

THE MOVE TO VIENNA

3

4

THE FINAL YEARS

A MUSICAL
PRODIGY

A Musical Family

On January 27, 1756, a boy was born who would become one of the greatest musicians of all time. He is known today as Wolfgang Amadeus Mozart. His family lived in Salzburg, in modern-day Austria, where his father worked as a musician in the Prince Archbishop's orchestra.

Salzburg was about 150 miles (240 km) from Vienna and was the capital of the Salzburg region of Austria. The word "*salzburg*" means "salt mountain." The city takes its name from the salt mined from the mountains nearby. When Mozart was born, the city was ruled by Prince Archbishop Sigismund Christoph von Schrattenbach, who had a palace overlooking the town.

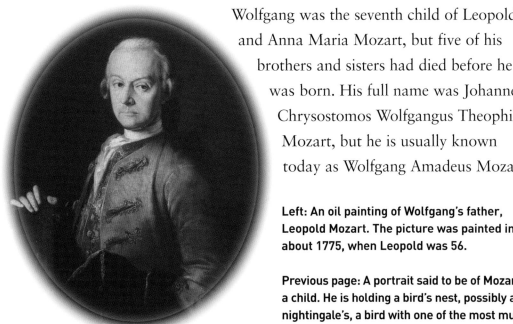

Wolfgang was the seventh child of Leopold and Anna Maria Mozart, but five of his brothers and sisters had died before he was born. His full name was Johannes Chrysostomos Wolfgangus Theophilus Mozart, but he is usually known today as Wolfgang Amadeus Mozart.

Left: An oil painting of Wolfgang's father, Leopold Mozart. The picture was painted in about 1775, when Leopold was 56.

Previous page: A portrait said to be of Mozart as a child. He is holding a bird's nest, possibly a nightingale's, a bird with one of the most musical songs. As an adult, Mozart kept a pet starling.

November 14, 1719
Leopold Mozart is born in Augsburg, Bavaria, in modern Germany.

1747
Leopold marries Anna Maria Pertl (born 1720).

Right: The house on the Getreidegasse in Salzburg where Wolfgang was born. The building (in the middle) is now a museum devoted to his life and work.

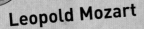

Leopold Mozart

Wolfgang's father played the violin at the court of the Prince Archbishop. He also composed some music, and taught young people the violin. He wrote a book, *Violin School*, which was published in 1756, the year Wolfgang was born. It became well known across Europe as a method for learning the violin.

The names Theophilus and Amadeus have the same meaning: "loved by God." Like most Austrians at the time, the Mozarts were Catholics. Wolfgang had a sister, Maria Anna, who was four years older than he was, and was known in the family as "Nannerl." The two children grew up in a house on Getreidegasse ("Cereal Lane"), where they lived comfortably on their father's income from the Prince Archbishop's court.

The Mozarts were a close and happy family. Although giving birth to Wolfgang had left his mother very weak, she was devoted to her two children. Leopold was very proud of Wolfgang and Maria Anna and took a great interest in their upbringing. Since he was a musician, there was always music being played in the Mozart household. Leopold's friends, who were often fellow musicians, frequently came to visit, and brought their musical instruments with them.

July 30, 1751
The Mozarts' first surviving child, Maria Anna (Nannerl) Mozart, is born.

January 27, 1756
Wolfgang Amadeus Mozart is born in Salzburg, in modern Austria.

Austrian Life

When Mozart was born, Austria was an important center of European political and cultural life. The capital, Vienna, was a rich and busy city from which Emperor Francis I (1745–65) held power over a collection of states, called the Holy Roman Empire, which covered a large part of central Europe. The empire had been ruled for centuries by the Habsburg family of Austria.

In fact the heir to the Habsburg throne was Francis's wife, Maria Theresia, Archduchess of Austria, but as a woman she could never be crowned Holy Roman Emperor. Although her son, Joseph II (1765–90), took the title after her husband's death, she held the real power until her death in 1780. At the heart of this powerful network of states, which included Bohemia, Belgium, Moravia, Hungary, and much of Germany, Austria was very wealthy.

Below: The Augarten in Vienna was opened to the public in 1775. This painting by Johann Ziegler shows families strolling through the gardens.

July 1756
Leopold Mozart publishes his book, *Violin School*, a method for teaching and learning to play the violin.

August 1756
The Seven Years' War begins, with Prussia and Britain fighting against France, Austria, and Russia.

Its cities became places where most people had a good standard of living and could afford some luxuries that previously only the aristocracy had had time and money to enjoy. There was a growing middle class, made up of people, like the Mozarts, with some education and some money to spend.

In Vienna in particular, people were looking for things to do with their leisure time. Public parks and gardens were opened. Going out to the theater or concert hall became a part of everyday life for many ordinary citizens. For the first time, people had the opportunity to see plays and to hear music that had previously only been performed in palaces and courts. Entertainment became big business, making some people rich and others famous.

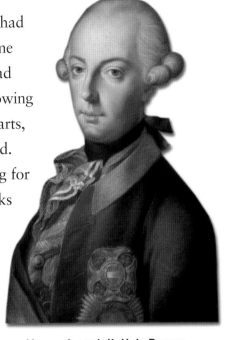

Above: Joseph II, Holy Roman Emperor, was an enthusiastic musician, and later took a keen interest in Mozart and his music.

For the wealthy, it was important to be seen keeping up with the latest fashions. Men wore brightly colored knee-breeches and jackets, with frilled shirts and buckled shoes, and some had wigs tied back with ribbons. Women wore full-length dresses, sometimes with hoops inside, known as a crinoline, to make them wider, and wore tall wigs. Both men and women used makeup to make their faces paler, and sometimes also added "beauty spots."

Transportation was becoming available to more people, and the streets of the cities were busy with horse-drawn carriages. Some of the wealthy could afford to have their own carriage; others could hire one for their journey. Traveling was popular with the rich, who might even visit other countries.

November 5, 1757
Frederick II of Prussia defeats Austria and France at the Battle of Rossbach during the Seven Years' War.

November 25, 1758
In America, John Forbes and George Washington capture Fort Duquesne (modern Pittsburgh) from the French.

Music Lessons

Most children of middle-class families learned to play a musical instrument. As Leopold was a professional musician, he encouraged his children's interest in music from a very early age. Nannerl was seven years old when she started music lessons, and three-year-old Wolfgang was eager to learn, too.

Even as a baby, Wolfgang would have heard music every day, as his father practiced at home. In addition to Leopold's violin, the family owned a harpsichord, a keyboard instrument similar to a piano. In a harpsichord, however, the strings are plucked to make the sounds, whereas in a piano they are struck with wooden hammers. Wolfgang must have enjoyed hearing all the music in the household. At only three years old, he was already picking out notes on the keyboard.

When Nannerl was seven years old, Leopold started teaching her the harpsichord and the clavichord, a keyboard instrument a bit like a small piano. Leopold gave her a music book in which she could write down the pieces that she was learning to play. Nannerl was a fine student, and soon became a good keyboard player. Wolfgang would have heard her practicing her pieces, and he was fascinated.

Showing off

Wolfgang enjoyed showing off his musical abilities in public. People were amazed to see such a small child play the harpsichord so impressively, but he also had a few party tricks to entertain them. He would play pieces from memory, and sometimes blindfolded or with the keyboard covered.

April 14, 1759

The composer George Frideric Handel dies in London. He was one of the most famous musicians of his time.

c. 1759

Leopold starts to give Wolfgang music lessons. ("c." is an abbreviation of "circa," meaning "about.")

Left: A piece of music written by Mozart when he was about seven years old. It is written to be played on a keyboard instrument such as a piano or harpsichord.

Leopold realized that Wolfgang was serious about learning music and started teaching him to play the harpsichord. He learned fast and was soon playing pieces from his sister's music books. By the time he was five, Wolfgang was not only able to play the keyboard well, but was also improvising (making up music as he played), and starting to compose some pieces of music of his own. These were short pieces for the harpsichord, which his father helped him to write down. These first pieces were the beginning of his career as a composer. When he was six, Wolfgang also began to learn to play the violin.

It was obvious to Leopold that his children were very gifted musicians, and that Wolfgang in particular was a prodigy. "Prodigy" means a young person with amazing talent. Leopold could see that Wolfgang was going to follow in his father's footsteps and become a professional musician. Visitors to the Mozart home were astonished by the children's music-making.

1759
John Harrison makes a clock that will win a prize for being accurate enough to use at sea for measuring longitude.

1760
Britain defeats the French in North America, and all of Canada comes under British rule.

Everyday Life

Wolfgang and Nannerl did not go to school. They were taught all their lessons at home by their father. They spent much of their days practicing their music, but they were also taught reading, writing, and mathematics. They enjoyed their lessons, and were also allowed time to have fun playing with their toys and games. Even though Nannerl was four years older than Wolfgang, they got along well and played together often.

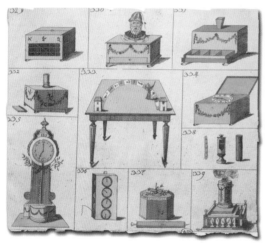

Above: A selection of mechanical toys, which were a new invention in the late 18th century. Some worked by turning a handle; others by winding a spring.

When they got up in the morning, the children would wash and get dressed. The flush toilet had not been invented yet, and toilets at that time emptied into a cesspit under the house which had to be emptied from time to time. There was no running water in houses either, so people had a washstand in their room with a jug of water and a bowl to wash in.

The daily routine for children of middle-class families involved either going to school, or, like the Mozarts, having lessons with a private tutor at home. For the younger children, there were educational toys and games, such as wooden bricks with letters printed on them, and picture books and cards to teach the alphabet.

September 1, 1761
Mozart makes probably his first appearance on stage, singing in a play in front of the Prince Archbishop.

January 1762
Wolfgang and Nannerl give their first public performances, in Munich, Germany.

When their lessons were over, children had a chance to play. They might own dolls to dress up, and many also had fine dollhouses with miniature furniture, or a model farm. Toy theaters made out of cardboard, in which children could play out stories with cutout figures, were also popular. Children could also have fun with wooden toy soldiers or ball games, and rolled hoops along the ground.

Wolfgang loved ball games all his life, and even as an adult he was fascinated by the new mechanical toys that were appearing. There were jack-in-the-boxes, steam engines, clockwork animals and people, and even some toys that played music.

What Mozart would have worn

When Mozart was a child, children wore clothes that were miniature versions of their parents'. Boys were dressed in knee-breeches and jackets, and even wore wigs. Girls had wide full-length dresses just like their mothers'. Wealthier parents had portraits painted of their children in their best outfits.

Right: Portraits of Wolfgang, seven, and Nannerl Mozart, eleven, in outfits given to them by the Empress Maria Theresia.

February 10, 1763
The Seven Years' War ends. Britain, France, and Spain sign a treaty known as the Treaty of Paris.

1763
Wolfgang, Nannerl, and Leopold Mozart start on a grand tour of Europe, which lasts until 1766.

The Mozarts on Tour

In 1762, Leopold Mozart took his children on a tour to show off their musical talents. He was not only proud of his children, but also realized he could make money and become famous from their music-making. Wolfgang was six, and Nannerl was ten. They visited Munich, where they performed for Prince Maximillian Joseph III, and then gave a public concert in Linz before going on to Vienna to play for Empress Maria Theresia herself at the Schönbrunn Palace. The trip was an enormous success, and news of the brilliant Mozart children spread fast.

In 1763, the Mozarts set off on a grand tour of Europe, visiting royal courts and palaces in Bavaria, Brussels, Paris, Versailles, and London, and returning via Amsterdam, several cities in Switzerland, and Munich once more before going home to Salzburg in 1766. Traveling long distances was slow, uncomfortable, and risky—in November 1765, for example, Wolfgang suffered from typhoid and nearly died.

Right: Nannerl kept a diary while the Mozarts were on tour. In it she wrote about all the places they visited and what happened there.

ENGLAND

London

Amsterdam

Brussels

GERMANY

FRANCE

Mannheim

Paris

Versailles

Prague

BAVARIA

Brno

AUSTRIA

Vienna

Linz

SWITZERLAND

Munich

Schönbrunn

Salzburg

Esterházy

Venice

Milan

This map of Europe shows some of the places Mozart visited on his tours. Europe in the 18th century was a very different place from the Europe of today. Much of central Europe was made up of small countries and regions that were all part of the Holy Roman Empire, ruled from Vienna. Royal families and noblemen ruled over different regions, and were often at war with one another. Their fighting also spread beyond Europe: for example, Britain and France were fighting for land in North America.

ITALY

Rome

Left: The splendid Palace of Versailles was home to the kings of France starting in 1682. The Mozart family performed there several times for King Louis XV (1715–74) and Queen Marie.

PERFORMING FOR KINGS AND EMPERORS

When Mozart was six he played for Emperor Francis I and Empress Maria Theresia in Vienna. They were delighted to see such a small boy play so well. Wolfgang was not old enough to understand how important these people were and at one point, so the story goes, he jumped onto the empress's lap and gave her a kiss. This French painting from 1763–4 shows Wolfgang sitting at the harpsichord, with his sister Nannerl singing and his father playing the violin.

The Young Composer

The tours across Europe, between 1762 and 1766, were hard work, but they established Wolfgang's reputation as a musician throughout Europe. Audiences were charmed by this musical family, and in particular by the boy who could play the harpsichord with such immense talent. Wolfgang had been writing his own simple musical compositions since he was five, and as he grew older his compositions became increasingly complex.

When Mozart had begun composing, he probably just made up tunes while playing the harpsichord, trying them out before he wrote them down. As he grew in confidence and skill, he was able to hear the music in his head and write it straight onto paper. In 1764, two sets of his pieces for violin and piano were published in Paris. These were his first published compositions. Mozart also learned about other instruments so that he could write music for them. By the time he returned from his tour in 1766, he had even written several pieces for whole orchestras, and some of them had been performed when the family was staying in London. While there, he had also taken singing lessons and written some vocal music (pieces for singers).

K (Köchel) numbers

Pieces of music are often listed in the order written by the composer. To help tell similar pieces from one another, they are usually given numbers, such as *Opus 1* (Latin for "work one"). In the late 19th century, the Austrian scholar Ludwig Köchel made a catalog of all Mozart's music, giving each piece a number. Today, we still use these "Köchel numbers" to refer to Mozart's music, for example: *La Finta Semplice* K51.

August 18, 1765

The Holy Roman Emperor Francis I dies. Joseph II becomes emperor, ruling with his mother, Maria Theresia.

1768

Mozart composes two operas, *La Finta Semplice* and *Bastien und Bastienne*.

Left: Mozart's first published pieces were two sets of sonatas for piano and violin, which he wrote in Paris in 1764. The picture shows the cover of the first set. Shops would sell the music to people who wanted to play it at home.

After long years of traveling, the Mozarts settled in Austria for a couple of years. While staying in Vienna in 1768, Mozart set to music the words of the Catholic Mass, and the piece was performed before the royal family. He also wrote two operas, *Bastien und Bastienne* ("Bastien and Bastienne") and *La Finta Semplice* ("The Pretend Simpleton"), which were first performed in 1768 and 1769. Operas were usually performed in Italian, as opera had begun in Italy in the early 1600s. Italy was where Wolfgang and his father toured next, from December 1769 to March 1771, and from August to December 1771. Wolfgang made the most of this opportunity to study music by Italian composers. The Italians liked his music, especially the operas *Mitridate* and *Ascanio in Alba*, which were performed in Milan in 1770 and 1771.

On their return to Salzburg in late 1771, life started to change for Wolfgang. At the age of 15, he was no longer a child prodigy: he needed to prove that he could make a living in the adult world and gain some independence from his father. So Wolfgang decided to start looking for a job.

1769–73

Wolfgang and Leopold make three trips to Italy. Wolfgang is given a medal by Pope Clemens XIV.

December 16, 1770

The great composer Ludwig van Beethoven is born in Bonn, Germany.

CONCERT
MASTER

2

First Job

Leopold was still employed by the Prince Archbishop of Salzburg, Sigismund von Schrattenbach. The Prince Archbishop appreciated the Mozart family's talents and allowed Leopold to take time off to travel, but all that changed when the archbishop died in 1771. The new Prince Archbishop, Hieronymous Colloredo, thought of the musicians in his court as servants and was not happy about them being absent from Salzburg. In August 1772, the archbishop offered Wolfgang a job as Konzertmeister (concert master).

Wolfgang accepted the job, and for the next few years he was based in Salzburg. The courts of 18th-century noblemen usually employed musicians, and even whole orchestras, to give concerts. Mozart's duties included composing church music, leading the Prince Archbishop's orchestra as the principal violinist, and organizing rehearsals.

However, Wolfgang was ambitious and both he and his father felt that the job was not going to give him the opportunities he wanted. He was too good a musician and composer to be happy in such a junior post.

Previous page: Mozart at about 21 years old, wearing the insignia of the Order of the Golden Spur. He was given this award in Italy by Pope Clemens XIV in 1770.

Music for the church

Music was an important part of services in churches. The larger churches had a choir and an organist, and some even had orchestras. Hymns and psalms were sung, and sometimes entire services were set to music. Mozart composed several pieces for the cathedral at Salzburg during his time as Konzertmeister. He was a Catholic and always enjoyed composing religious music.

1771

Leopold's employer, Prince Archbishop von Schrattenbach, dies.

August 9, 1772

Mozart gets his first job. He is made Konzertmeister at Prince Archbishop Colloredo's court.

Salzburg was too small to attract large audiences, and Wolfgang felt his talent was being wasted. Besides, if he could get a job in one of the big cities, he would also have more opportunity to go out and enjoy himself.

Later that year, Leopold and Wolfgang managed to persuade the archbishop to let them travel to Italy once more. Mozart had been commissioned to write an opera for the Milan opera house, and they traveled to Milan for the first performance of *Lucio Silla* on December 26, 1772. This was another success and confirmed Mozart's reputation as an opera composer in Italy.

The next year, the Mozarts visited Vienna, looking for better employment. However, Wolfgang was still considered too young to hold a more senior post, and they were unsuccessful. Mozart was eager to make a name for himself as a composer. He also wanted to write more operas, which were very popular in the big cities, but there was no regular opera company in Salzburg. The commissions he got to write operas were coming from outside Salzburg, and he had to write these in addition to his work in the Prince Archbishop's court. He had been asked to write an opera for the carnival season in Munich, and began working on *La Finta Giardiniera* ("The Pretend Gardener") in 1774.

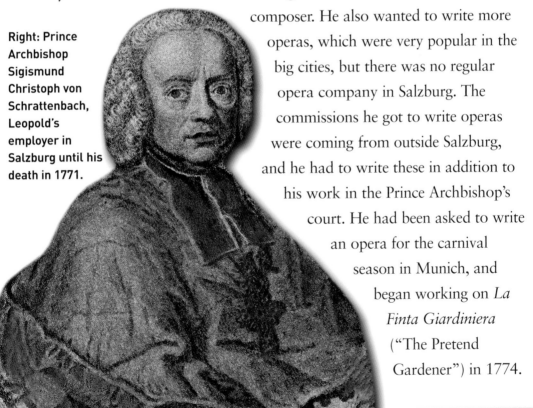

Right: Prince Archbishop Sigismund Christoph von Schrattenbach, Leopold's employer in Salzburg until his death in 1771.

1773
Mozart travels to Vienna, looking for a better post.

May 10, 1774
Louis XV of France dies. His grandson, Louis XVI, becomes king of France.

Prince Archbishop's Court

Mozart's time as Konzertmeister for Prince Archbishop Colloredo was not particularly happy. Although he was working as a musician and composing his first important pieces, Wolfgang missed being in the public eye. The Prince Archbishop was also a hard taskmaster.

Colloredo insisted that Mozart should be available at the court, and gave him little free time. However, in 1775 Mozart did manage to get permission to go to Munich for the first performance of his opera *La Finta Giardiniera*.

During his time as Konzertmeister, Wolfgang composed a lot of music for the court musicians. Much of it was religious music for services in the cathedral. Other important pieces were symphonies (for orchestra), concertos (for a solo instrument and orchestra), and sonatas (for solo piano or for piano and violin).

Below: Today's Mozart Festival Orchestra performing as musicians would have done in Mozart's time, by candlelight and wearing 18th-century fashions.

January 1775
Mozart's opera *La Finta Giardiniera* is performed. It is his first success as an opera composer outside Italy.

February 1775
Peasants in Bohemia, part of the Austrian Empire, start a protest against their masters.

Left: The Prince Archbishop's Palace was perched on a rock overlooking Salzburg. In the foreground of this picture are washerwomen doing laundry in the river.

Patronage

Professional musicians up to Mozart's time were nearly all employed by the church or royalty. The royal families paid for musicians to entertain them and their guests. This system was known as patronage, and the people who paid for the music were known as patrons.

Mozart wrote five violin concertos in his life, and all of them were composed during his time in Salzburg. The first of his great piano concertos also came from this period, as well as a number of fine symphonies. These compositions showed that Mozart had learned a lot on his travels. The pieces were well received, and he was now recognized as an important composer in Salzburg. Even more, he was not content just to write music similar to that of the other composers of the time, but was developing his own style of composition and producing some truly original pieces. His music was fresh and modern, but also very expressive of Mozart's sensitive and outgoing personality.

Wolfgang was increasingly dissatisfied in Salzburg. He knew he could make a great name for himself as a composer if he could find a more suitable job and a wider audience. But while he was employed by the Archbishop, his music was seldom performed outside Salzburg. Leopold was unhappy with this situation too, and wanted his son to have the fame he thought he deserved.

1775
The American Revolution against British rule begins.

July 4, 1776
The American Declaration of Independence is approved by the Continental Congress.

Musical Instruments

There are all sorts of different musical instruments, which are usually divided into "families" of similar instruments: strings, woodwinds, brass, percussion, and keyboard instruments. Instruments can be played on their own or in groups. An orchestra is a large group that can include instruments from all the musical families, but is almost always made up mainly of stringed instruments. As new instruments were invented, composers wrote music that used these new sounds. New technology made instruments such as the clarinet and trumpet easier to play, so they were included in orchestral music more often.

STRINGED INSTRUMENTS

In the 18th century, very fine stringed instruments were being made, such as this violin (left) by Omobono Stradivari, one of the famous family of Italian violin makers. The violin is the smallest and highest-sounding of the stringed instruments. The next smallest, and slightly lower in sound, is the viola. To play the lower notes, there are the cello and the double bass. In a modern orchestra there can be as many as fifty string players, but in Mozart's time there were normally only a few violins, two or three violas and cellos, and one double bass.

WOODWINDS, BRASS, AND PERCUSSION

The woodwind instruments are so called because they are played by blowing into them and were made of wood until the invention of plastics. The woodwind family includes the flute, which plays the high notes, through the oboe and clarinet, and down to the bassoon, which plays the bottom notes. The picture (right) shows an 18th-century clarinet, which was just beginning to appear in orchestras in Mozart's day. At this time, composers sometimes included brass instruments, such as trumpets, horns, and trombones, and these soon became regular members of the orchestra. Finally there is the percussion family. This family includes all sorts of drums, especially the timpani (or kettledrums), which look like enormous cooking pots. There are also plates of metal clashed together called cymbals, and the metal triangle.

Left: There are lots of different kinds of music for an orchestra, but the most common is the symphony, a piece in several sections, or movements. In this 18th-century engraving, you can see a viola-player sitting at the front, and facing him, from left to right, a viola da gamba (a type of viola), oboe, flute, double bass, violins, and harpsichord.

KEYBOARD INSTRUMENTS

Most people are familiar with the piano, or to give it its full name, pianoforte (Italian for "soft loud"). The piano is a member of the keyboard family, as it is played by pressing keys to operate a mechanism that produces the sound. It was invented at the beginning of the 18th century, but only really became popular in Mozart's time. Other keyboard instruments include the organ, harpsichord, and clavichord. Until the piano was invented, the harpsichord was the most common keyboard instrument. Although he learned to play the more old-fashioned harpsichord as a child, Mozart preferred the piano, and wrote some of the first music that explored the possibilities of the new instrument. This picture shows Mozart's own piano.

Frustrating Times

Mozart celebrated his 21st birthday on January 27, 1777. Both he and Nannerl were still living at home with their parents, and Wolfgang was doing a job that he found boring and unrewarding. He felt increasingly trapped and frustrated.

Leopold asked his employer several times if the Mozarts could be allowed to travel to find better prospects for Wolfgang. Each time, Colloredo refused. Eventually, when Wolfgang himself asked, the Archbishop agreed to let them go. However, Leopold had to stay in Salzburg as the Archbishop threatened to fire him if he left. In any case, Leopold was suffering with rheumatism and was not well enough to travel. So, in 1777, Mozart and his mother went to Munich, where Wolfgang had already had some success with his opera *La Finta Giardiniera*.

Left: A view of the Port Royal in Paris in the 18th century. Paris was a busy city, and boats carried goods in from the coast up the River Seine. It was also one of the cultural centers of Europe, and famous for its fine orchestras.

1777
Mozart and his mother set off to look for a new job for him in Munich, Mannheim, and Paris.

January 1778
Mozart meets the singer Aloysia Weber in Mannheim.

Right: A portrait of Anna Maria Mozart, Wolfgang's
mother, who died in Paris in 1778.

Unfortunately, Mozart found no
suitable job prospects in Munich, so
he and his mother traveled on to
Mannheim. Wolfgang enjoyed
Mannheim for two reasons: he got
along well with the musicians in the
orchestra and was very impressed by
the sound they made, but more
importantly he met a singer and pianist
named Aloysia Weber and immediately fell in
love with her. This was his first serious love. He
would have been happy to stay in Mannheim, but he could not find a job.

Leopold was stage-managing their tour from home, and suggested in a
letter to them that they should try their luck in Paris. This turned out to be
a disaster. Mozart did not get along well with the musicians in Paris and
was not offered any work. Then, his mother fell ill with a fever and died
there in July 1778. Wolfgang was grief-stricken and felt that his father
blamed him for the death. His one consolation was writing letters to Aloysia.

Mozart knew that he had to return home to Salzburg. It was not
something he was looking forward to, as he would have to face his father's
disappointment and grief as well as his old job at Colloredo's court.
Delaying his return, he stopped off in Mannheim once again to stay with
Aloysia and her family. But even there he was to be disappointed. Aloysia
let him know that she did not love him.

1778
The opera house of La Scala opens in
Milan. It was one of many opera
houses built in the 18th century.

July 3, 1778
Anna Maria Mozart dies in Paris.

Above: A portrait of the Mozarts painted in 1780–81. Leopold can be seen with his violin, with Nannerl and Wolfgang at the piano. Anna Maria's portrait is hanging on the wall behind them.

Eventually, in January 1779, Mozart returned to Salzburg. His father was disappointed with him for not finding a job, and the whole family was missing their mother. After hearing the orchestras at Mannheim and Paris, Mozart found the musicians at Salzburg rather second-rate. Stuck in a job he disliked, suffering from the death of his mother, made to feel guilty about it by his father, and devastated by his failed affair with Aloysia, it was difficult for Mozart to find inspiration. But he still managed to compose a great deal, including a couple of excellent symphonies, his "Coronation" Mass, and the *Sinfonia Concertante* for violin and viola.

Mozart's relationship with his father was becoming difficult as he tried to assert his independence. They argued about how Wolfgang could improve his career, and the atmosphere in the Mozart home was gloomy.

January 1779
Mozart returns to Salzburg.

1780
Empress Maria Theresia of Austria dies. Joseph II becomes sole ruler of Austria.

Then, in 1780, things started to change for the better. Mozart was asked to write another opera to be performed in Munich, and he started work immediately on *Idomeneo*, the story of a king of ancient Crete. At the same time, it was announced that Joseph II was to become sole ruler of Austria after the death of his mother, Maria Theresia, with whom he had been co-ruler. This was exciting news for Mozart, as Joseph enjoyed music and the theater, and might be a generous patron.

The first performance of *Idomeneo* was January 29, 1781, just before the coronation of the new emperor. As the Prince Archbishop went to Vienna for the ceremony, Mozart was able to get away to Munich to direct his opera. It was a huge success, and Wolfgang felt that he was finally winning respect.

However, his happiness did not last long. He was summoned to Vienna by his employer, and then made to eat and sleep in the servants' quarters. This was the last straw for Mozart, who had a fierce argument with the Prince Archbishop. It is not clear whether he resigned from his job or was fired, but his time at the Salzburg court was definitely over.

Mozart decided to stay on in Vienna to find work. The Weber family had a house there and offered to let Mozart stay with them. Aloysia was now married, but Wolfgang was very attracted to her younger sister, Constanze.

Other composers

Mozart admired the work of other composers of his day, and some of them were friends of his. He knew Michael Haydn (1737–1806) and later became good friends with his brother Joseph Haydn (1732–1809). Other composers he met included Antonio Salieri (1750–1825), who worked at Joseph II's court, and Muzio Clementi (1752–1832). Among Mozart's pupils was a composer called Franz Xaver Süssmayr, who finished Mozart's last work.

January 29, 1781
Mozart's opera *Idomeneo* premieres in Munich.

May or June 1781
Mozart leaves Archbishop Colloredo's employment.

THE MOVE TO VIENNA

3

A Break for Independence

Leaving the Prince Archbishop's court was a huge step for Mozart. He had gotten away from a job that he hated and was now living in the great city of Vienna, where he hoped to find all the opportunities he was looking for. He had also made an important break with his father and shown that he was capable of making decisions on his own.

Leopold did not respond well to Wolfgang's decision. He wrote to his son saying he thought the move to Vienna was a mistake, especially as Mozart had no job to go to. The letters between them were much less friendly than they had been before. However, Wolfgang was delighted with his new independence and launched himself enthusiastically into city life. He went to the theater and opera, and mixed with influential people and musicians. His plan was to work as a freelance musician, earning his money by playing the piano, teaching music, and composing. That way, he could make a living without having to find a full-time job.

Left: A 19th-century painting depicting a scene from *Die Entführung aus dem Serail*, showing the exotic Turkish costumes and stage scenery.

Previous page: Mozart as a young man. As he grew up, he felt the need to get away from Salzburg and his family, and to have the freedom to compose as he wanted.

May 1781
Mozart moves into the Webers' house in Vienna.

1781
The American Revolution draws to an end after the British surrender at Yorktown.

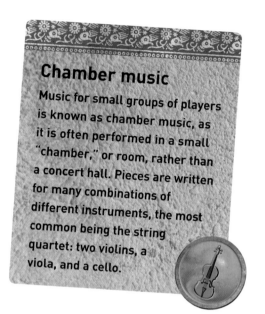

Chamber music

Music for small groups of players is known as chamber music, as it is often performed in a small "chamber," or room, rather than a concert hall. Pieces are written for many combinations of different instruments, the most common being the string quartet: two violins, a viola, and a cello.

Above: A poster advertising the first performance of *Die Entführung aus dem Serail* in July 1782 at the Burgtheater, Vienna.

It was very unusual for musicians not to be employed by the church or courts, and it was hard for Mozart to make money. He gave music lessons, and was paid to compose a few pieces, but it was not enough for him to live on. Mozart knew many of Vienna's nobles from his time as a child performer, but he had no reputation in the city as an adult composer. If it had not been for the Webers, who provided him with an inexpensive room and food, he could not have remained in Vienna for long.

Slowly, however, his talent won through and he began to make a name for himself in Vienna. He was asked to play the piano in concerts, and commissioned to compose more music. The big break came for him with the performance of his *Die Entführung aus dem Serail* ("The Abduction from the Harem") at the Burgtheater in Vienna. This was a singspiel, a type of opera performed in German with spoken parts as well as singing. The opera was a great success with the audiences in Vienna when it premiered in July 1782. Now Mozart felt that he had succeeded in becoming a freelance composer.

July 1781
Mozart receives the libretto of *Die Entführung aus dem Serail* and starts to compose the music.

1781
Austria and Russia sign a treaty, joining forces with the aim of eventually driving the Turks out of Europe.

Life as a freelance musician was not always as glamorous as the success of *Die Entführung*. Mozart knew that the public would soon forget him if he did not continue producing new music that they liked. He had to work very hard to maintain his reputation and to earn enough money to live on.

What Mozart wanted to do more than anything was compose, especially operas. But to do this he had to find people who would pay him to compose, and a way to sell his music. Sometimes wealthy music-lovers would commission him to write pieces for them, and in return, Mozart would dedicate the music to them. He would sometimes be paid to write a piece for a particular performer to play or sing in a concert, and when pieces he had written were played publicly, he was also paid a fee. He took most of his music to publishers so that it could be printed and sold to the public.

Opera was more difficult to sell. It took a long time to write, and involved a lot of performers and back-stage workers. This was expensive, and the theater putting on the opera had to be sure that it was going to be a success.

Above: Wolfgang and his father kept in touch by letter after he left Salzburg. This letter was written by Mozart in 1781. Leopold's letters to his son have been lost, but Wolfgang's replies make it clear that his father's words were harsh for a while after the move to Vienna.

May 9, 1782

Peace talks open in France between the United States and Britain.

July 1782

Mozart's *Die Entführung aus dem Serail* premieres in Vienna. It is a great success.

They would only pay composers like Mozart to write operas if they knew that they would attract big audiences.

In order to keep money coming in regularly, Wolfgang had to continue to give music lessons and to play the piano in concerts. He knew he could not rely on the Webers' hospitality forever, and would have to find a home for himself. Besides, he was thinking about getting married.

By now, he had gotten over the disappointment of being turned down by Aloysia and, while living with the Weber family, he had become close to her sister, Constanze. She was just 19 years old, and Mozart was 25. During his first year in Vienna, their friendship turned into love, and Wolfgang felt it was time for them to get married.

Letters home

Mozart spent a lot of time away from his family, and kept in touch by letter. Many of his letters to his family have been kept so that we can read them today, and they make fascinating reading. They contain lots of family news, and show that Wolfgang had a very good—and rude!—sense of humor.

Right: A music teacher giving a piano lesson. The children of aristocratic families were expected to be able to play a musical instrument, and many professional musicians gave music lessons.

August 4, 1782
Mozart marries Constanze Weber in St. Stephen's Cathedral, Vienna.

December 1782
Wolfgang and Constanze move to a new apartment in Vienna.

Setting up House

The year 1782 was a very important one for Mozart. At the age of 26, he had established himself as a composer and pianist in Vienna, especially with the success of *Die Entführung*. Just as importantly for him, it was also the year when he set up a home for himself. On August 4, he married Constanze in St. Stephen's Cathedral in Vienna.

Mozart's father had been hurt when Wolfgang moved to Vienna against his advice—and now his son was marrying against his advice as well. He did not approve of Constanze, and hinted that she only wanted Wolfgang's money. Mozart's letters home reveal that father and son were not getting along, and relations between them were so bad that Leopold and Nannerl were not invited to the wedding. However, Mozart was happy with his new life. He was enjoying his work and was now making enough money to live comfortably. He and Constanze were starting a family: in June 1783, Constanze gave birth to a baby boy, Raimund Leopold.

Left: Mozart's wife, Constanze (1762–1842). She and Wolfgang married against his father's wishes, but she was a loving wife and a constant support to him in his musical career. She, too, came from a musical family, and was able both to help him with his composing and manage the household.

June 17, 1783
The Mozarts' first child, Raimund Leopold, is born.

July 1783
Wolfgang and Constanze travel to Salzburg to visit Leopold and Nannerl.

Mozart was busy composing piano concertos, songs, string quartets, and several serenades for social occasions. A serenade is a piece of music written for an evening performance. Mozart was now very much a part of the social life in Vienna. He was making some influential friends in the musical and theater world, and among the aristocrats who supported the arts.

In July, Wolfgang and Constanze left baby Raimund in Vienna while they traveled to Salzburg to see Nannerl and Leopold. During the visit relations were strained between Nannerl and Constanze, as Nannerl never really liked her brother's wife. While Wolfgang and Constanze were away from home, Raimund Leopold died of what was described as an "intestinal cramp." Without the benefits of modern medicine, it was not uncommon for babies to die. Still, Wolfgang and Constanze must have been very sad.

In late October, the couple left Salzburg, probably relieved to be getting back to Vienna. On the way back, they stopped in Linz, where Mozart gave a concert. In the space of only a few days, he wrote and rehearsed a symphony for the occasion, now known as the "Linz" symphony, K425.

Below: The city of Linz, between Salzburg and Vienna, where Mozart composed a symphony at incredible speed.

August 1783
Raimund Leopold dies.

September 3, 1783
Britain agrees to recognize American independence. The two countries sign treaties called the Peace of Paris.

The Age of Enlightenment

Mozart lived in an age when the world was changing rapidly. The growth of industry and factories was bringing people into the cities to find work, and trade was making some of them wealthy. Scientists had made discoveries that changed people's ideas about mankind's place in the world, and made them question whether the Church and royal families should have so much power. Historians call this period the "Age of Enlightenment," or the "Age of Reason."

Right: The French writer Pierre Augustin Caron de Beaumarchais wrote the play *The Marriage of Figaro*, which Mozart made into an opera. The story is about some servants who get the better of their masters.

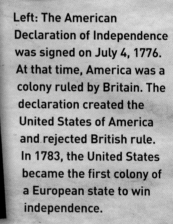

Left: The American Declaration of Independence was signed on July 4, 1776. At that time, America was a colony ruled by Britain. The declaration created the United States of America and rejected British rule. In 1783, the United States became the first colony of a European state to win independence.

THE AGE OF REVOLUTIONS

When Mozart was born, Europe was ruled by kings, queens, and emperors. There were no elections to choose governments, and ordinary people had no say in how their countries were run. Religious leaders, such as the pope and the archbishops, wielded a lot of power. In the 18th century, writers and thinkers, such as Voltaire (1694–1778), Jean Jacques Rousseau (1712–78), and Denis Diderot (1713–84) in France, and Thomas Paine (1737–1809) in America, questioned the right of royal families to rule over their people. They believed that all men should be free and equal, and that ordinary people had rights, too. In many countries, there was a growing desire for change. Such ideas swiftly led to revolutions in America (1775–83) and France (1789–99), where the old rulers were toppled and new democratic governments set up.

Right: On July 14, 1789, a crowd attacked the prison of the Bastille in Paris. It was the first step in the French Revolution, which overthrew the monarchy in France. In 1793, King Louis XVI was executed, and France was declared a republic.

THE CLASSICAL STYLE

During the Age of Enlightenment, people were fascinated by the art, architecture, and writings of the classical civilizations of ancient Rome and Greece, where ideas about democracy and science had also been hotly debated. Artists and architects imitated the simple, elegant style of these times, and composers captured that elegance and simplicity in their music. Because of this, the arts of the Age of Enlightenment are often said to be in the classical style.

Left: The ancient Roman city of Pompeii was covered with ash from the eruption of the volcano Vesuvius in A.D. 79, but was rediscovered in 1748. The classical style of architecture there inspired architects and artists such as Piranesi (1720–78), who drew this picture of the ruins of Pompeii.

Mozart and Haydn

One of the attractions of Vienna for Mozart was that he felt at the heart of musical life. As well as performing and writing his own music, he could go to listen to other composers' music, too. Many of these composers were friends of his. One in particular became a lifelong friend, and inspired much of his music. Joseph Haydn (1732–1809) was 24 years older than Mozart, but the two musicians had a great deal in common. They were the two greatest composers of their time.

Mozart and Haydn probably met for the first time in 1781, but the connection between the two musicians started long before then. Haydn's younger brother Michael (1737–1806) was also a composer and had arrived in Salzburg when Mozart was a child. Mozart got along well with Michael and admired his music, and probably came across Joseph Haydn's music through him. Joseph heard about young Wolfgang and his music as his fame spread.

Right: Joseph Haydn at the height of his career. He wrote 104 symphonies, more than 80 string quartets, and literally hundreds of other pieces. His orchestra was so fond of him that the musicians nicknamed him "Papa" Haydn.

1783
American inventor Oliver Evans builds a mechanized flour mill, the first mill able to grind grain continuously.

1784
French writer Beaumarchais writes a play called *The Marriage of Figaro*.

"The greatest composer known to me in person or by name; he has taste and, what is more, the greatest knowledge of composition."

Joseph Haydn on Mozart

Haydn spent all his working life as a musician in the court at Esterházy in Hungary. He composed music of all sorts, but was especially famous for his symphonies and string quartets, which set the standard for music in the new classical style. Mozart was so impressed by Haydn's quartets that he was inspired to write some of his own, and in 1785 he dedicated a set of six string quartets to him. Haydn was equally impressed by Mozart's work.

The two soon became firm friends. It was not just a love of music that they shared. They both had a good sense of humor, which often shows in their music in the form of musical jokes and surprises, and enjoyed talking to one another.

Below: Billiards was a popular game in the taverns of Mozart's time. Both he and Haydn loved it, and were very good players.

August 1784
Nannerl marries a judge, Johann Baptist Berchtold zu Sonnenburg, and moves out of the family home.

1784
The English writer Samuel Johnson, creator of the first English dictionary, dies in London.

The Toast of the Town

After the difficult first couple of years as a freelance musician, Mozart knew that he had made a good decision in moving to Vienna. He was now kept busy composing and performing, and was regarded as one of the greatest musicians in the world. Constanze and he were happily married and living quite comfortably.

Vienna was exactly the right place for Mozart. Emperor Joseph II was an enthusiastic music-lover, and he gave his support to series of public concerts and operas performed in the Burgtheater in the center of town. Mozart was one of his favorite musicians, and royal approval helped build Wolfgang's reputation.

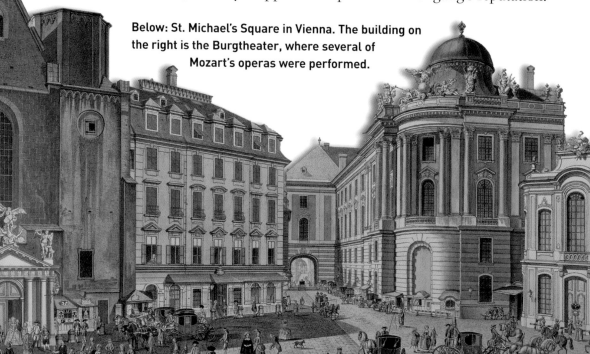

Below: St. Michael's Square in Vienna. The building on the right is the Burgtheater, where several of Mozart's operas were performed.

September 21, 1784
The Mozarts' second child, Carl Thomas (1784–1858), is born.

December 14, 1784
Mozart joins the Freemasons. A few months later, both his father and Joseph Haydn become Freemasons, too.

Mozart's music was much in demand. He was an excellent pianist, and performed several nights a week. The most important pieces he wrote at this time were the concertos for piano and orchestra, in which he could play the solo part. Rich patrons paid him to entertain at their houses, or compose music dedicated to them. Some of his music was published, and amateur musicians bought copies of his pieces from the music shops to play at home.

Above: Vienna was famous for its social life, which Mozart enjoyed greatly. As well as the theater, concerts, operas, and balls, Viennese gentlemen often went to the many cafés, as seen here.

By the mid-1780s, Mozart was famous and earning very well. However, he was not good at managing money, and was spending it as fast as he earned it while enjoying an expensive lifestyle. In September 1784, Constanze gave birth to their second son, Carl Thomas, and they moved to a bigger apartment on the fashionable Domgasse. Despite his success, Wolfgang was finding it difficult to keep up with all the bills.

The piano

Bartolomeo Cristofori, an Italian harpsichord maker, invented the piano at the beginning of the 18th century. Unlike the harpsichord, the piano is capable of playing both loudly and softly, so it is a much more expressive instrument. Some of the finest pianos were being made in Vienna, and Mozart played these at home and in the concert halls. He was an outstanding pianist, often improvising pieces on the piano during performances.

1785
Mozart dedicates six string quartets to his friend Joseph Haydn.

May 1, 1786
Mozart's opera *Le Nozze di Figaro* (The Marriage of Figaro) premieres at Vienna's Burgtheater.

Viennese Society

As he became more successful, Mozart was busier than ever. He spent most of the day composing or rehearsing, and the evenings performing in concerts. But he still managed to make time for other things. His family was important to him, and he even found time for some hobbies.

Mozart was proud of his family and wanted the best for them. Their new apartment was quite luxurious, and he employed servants to do the housework. When his father came to visit them in 1785, Mozart was able to show him how successful and happy he was, in an attempt to end the bad feeling between them. Nannerl had married the previous year, so she did not accompany her father on the trip. Leopold wrote to her about Wolfgang's success and happiness and he seemed thoroughly proud of his son.

Mozart had made many good friends in Vienna, and some of them introduced him to a society called the Freemasons, which he joined in 1784. His father and Joseph Haydn also joined a few months later.

Left: The 18th-century game of skittles was similar to today's tenpin bowling, but with nine "pins." The skittle alleys in the taverns and parks in Vienna were fashionable meeting places.

October 1786
The Mozarts' third child, Johann Thomas, is born. He dies a month later.

May 28, 1787
Mozart's father, Leopold, dies in Salzburg.

Right: In their secret rituals, Freemasons wear aprons which show symbols of the society: The Temple of Solomon between two columns, the sun and moon, a triangle, and the tools of the stonemason, the trade in which freemasonry may have its origins.

Freemasonry

The Freemasons are a society which still exists today. Only men can join, and they must follow a strict code of morals and perform secret rituals. Freemasons believe that all men should be treated as brothers: a belief that fit well with the ideas of the Age of Enlightenment.

Freemasonry became very important to Mozart, as the society's beliefs about human equality were very much what he believed, too. He made references to the symbols of freemasonry in some of his later operas. The Freemasons also gave him the chance to meet some rich and influential people. Mozart sometimes borrowed money from them.

Society in Vienna liked Mozart not only for his music, but also for his company. He was often the life and soul of a party, as he was charming and had a mischievous sense of humor. He even composed "musical jokes," pieces with wrong notes in them, or mimicking other composers' music.

The many taverns and cafés in Vienna were also favorite places for Mozart, especially if he could combine his drinking with a game of skittles or billiards. Wolfgang needed to unwind, as he was having to work harder and harder to earn enough money to maintain his standard of living.

September 17, 1787
The United States Constitution is signed.

October 29, 1787
Mozart's opera *Don Giovanni* premieres in Prague.

THE FINAL
YEARS

Money Worries

Vienna had turned out to be everything Mozart had hoped for. By the mid-1780s, he was happily married, thoroughly independent, and a famous composer. There was one ambition still outstanding. One reason why he had come to Vienna was to have a chance to compose more operas, but no opportunities had arisen since *Die Entführung*. In 1786, that was to change. But despite all his success, Mozart was still having problems with money.

Above: When Mozart visited Prague in 1787, he stayed in the Villa Betramka. His Symphony No. 38 K504 was written during his visit there, and has been given the nickname the "Prague" symphony.

Previous page: Constanze considered this portrait of Mozart to be the best likeness of him. It was painted by her sister Aloysia's husband, Joseph Lange, in 1789.

To his great happiness, in 1786, Mozart was commissioned to write an opera to be performed at the emperor's palace. The opera, *Der Schauspieldirektor* ("The Impresario"), was his first since *Die Entführung*, four years earlier. Later that year, he finished a comic opera in Italian, *Le Nozze di Figaro* ("The Marriage of Figaro"). It was performed in Vienna in May, and was a great success. Mozart had achieved his ambition to become famous as an opera composer. At the same time, he continued to perform and compose other music.

December 1787

Emperor Joseph II offers Mozart a job as "chamber musician."

December 1787

The Mozarts' fourth child, Theresia, is born.

Left: Masked balls were great social occasions in Vienna. Guests dressed up in costumes and wore masks. Mozart was especially fond of these balls and sometimes composed music for them.

Ludwig van Beethoven

In 1787 a composer came to Vienna to seek his fortune. His name was Ludwig van Beethoven (1770–1827). He wanted to take lessons with Mozart, but news came that his mother had died and he returned home. He came back to Vienna after Mozart's death.

Le Nozze di Figaro was played in opera houses outside Vienna, too, and he was invited to the first performance in Prague. While Mozart was there, he also gave concerts, wrote a symphony for the Prague orchestra, and was commissioned to write another opera, *Don Giovanni*.

When he and Constanze came back from Prague in 1787, they moved from their fashionable apartment on the Domgasse to a smaller and less expensive one in the Hauptstrasse. They had to save money because the income from Mozart's playing and composing was sometimes very good but could also be unreliable. Later in the year, Wolfgang was offered a part-time job as Kammermusicus ("chamber musician") by Emperor Joseph II. It was not an important post, mainly involving writing music for entertainment in the court, and the salary was not very large. But Mozart accepted the position gratefully. It gave him the much needed security of a regular income, as well as the official recognition that Mozart felt he deserved.

December 1787
The Mozarts move to a less expensive apartment on Vienna's Hauptstrasse.

June 1788
Theresia Mozart dies.

Left: Manuscript in Mozart's handwriting of *Eine Kleine Nachtmusik*. He did not consider this a very important piece, but it is now one of his best-known compositions.

Mozart was beginning to find it difficult to get big audiences for his concerts. In some ways, his father had been right to warn Wolfgang about going to Vienna. He had told Mozart that, even if he did become a successful composer, the public was always looking for something new, and it would be hard to stay popular. Although Mozart was still regarded very highly, his music was now thought of as unfashionable. At the same time, the Empire had gotten involved in a war against Turkey, so there was less public money to spend on music. Mozart was having to work even harder to make enough money.

There was also sadness at home. Constanze gave birth to two more children, Johann Thomas in 1786 and a girl, Theresia, in 1787. Both children survived only a few months. As a result of her pregnancies and the deaths of her children, Constanze was often ill. Wolfgang was overworked and tired. In May 1787, Mozart's father Leopold died. Even though the relationship between father and son had been strained at times after Wolfgang's move to Vienna, Leopold's death was a huge blow to him. For a while, Wolfgang felt overwhelmed by all his problems.

Nevertheless, he managed to continue working, composing several piano pieces, chamber music, and some orchestral pieces for the court at Schönbrunn.

1789

Steam engines are used for the first time to power a cotton factory in Manchester, England.

1789

Mozart travels to Prague, Dresden, Leipzig, and Berlin in search of work.

These included the serenades *Eine Kleine Nachtmusik* ("A Little Night Music") and *Ein Musikalischer Spass* ("A Musical Joke"), which poked fun at bad composers. However, most of his time was devoted to the opera for Prague. He finished *Don Giovanni* in 1787, and traveled to Prague for the first performance. Once again, this opera was a great success, which helped lift his spirits.

Below: Constanze Mozart suffered from periods of bad health and went to Baden, a spa town near Vienna, to rest and bathe in the mineral waters.

Librettos

A composer writing an opera sets the words of a play to music. Usually the words are specially written for the opera. The words are known as the libretto (Italian for "little book"), and the person who writes them is called the librettist. Mozart's librettists included Lorenzo Da Ponte (1749–1838), who wrote the librettos for *Le Nozze di Figaro*, *Don Giovanni*, and *Così fan Tutte*, and Emanuel Schikaneder (1751–1812), librettist of *Die Zauberflöte*.

July 14, 1789
Rioters storm the prison at the Bastille, in Paris. This marks the start of the French Revolution.

November 1789
The Mozarts' fifth child, Anna Maria, is born, and dies one hour later.

Opera

In about 1600, a new kind of entertainment appeared in Italy. It was a form of theater in which the actors sang the words while accompanied by instruments. This combination of drama and music is known as opera. From the very beginning, audiences loved operas. They became a fashionable entertainment and were performed all over Europe. Composers started to write new operas to meet the public demand. At first, these were in the same style as the first Italian operas and were sung in Italian, but slowly each country developed its own style and used its own language. Different kinds of operas also appeared. Some were based on classical myths and legends, while others were simple love stories. Just like plays for the theater, there were tragedies and comedies. In some operas, some of the words were spoken rather than sung. This sort of opera was known in Germany as singspiel ("sing play").

PUTTING ON AN OPERA

Operas involve a lot of people. First, there are the composer and librettist. Then there are set and costume designers. And, of course, there are musicians: a conductor and an orchestra to accompany the singers. The musicians in the orchestra are usually out of sight of the audience. They play in a special area called the orchestra pit (left). So that they cannot be seen, they often sit in darkness, and need lamps to see their music. In many operas there is a chorus made up of a group of singers. However, the stars are the solo singers. They play the leading parts in the story and sing the arias (Italian for "songs").

Left: Operas are often very spectacular. The scenery on the stage, or set, is specially designed for each opera. This is a set design for a performance of Mozart's *Le Nozze di Figaro*.

Right: The singers in an opera dress for their parts and wear stage makeup. For important performances, special clothes are made, like these costumes for a 1915 performance of *Le Nozze di Figaro*.

Below: Opera became so popular in the 18th century that opera houses were built in many cities. This drawing of La Scala opera house in Milan shows how big and luxurious they often are.

The Last Works

Mozart's *Don Giovanni* had been a huge success in Prague, but when it was put on in Vienna, audiences were not so enthusiastic. He was disappointed, especially as he was not being asked to perform in concerts either. Perhaps it was time for him to look outside Vienna for work again.

Don Giovanni.
Rappres.^t dal Signor Bassi.
Att. Ser.^{ta}

Above: This poster shows the famous singer Luigi Bassi, who played the title role of Don Giovanni in the first performance of Mozart's opera.

Before he went in search of better-paid work, Mozart spent time trying to organize concerts for himself. He was also doing some fine composing and, in the summer of 1788, wrote three symphonies: Symphony No. 39 K543, Symphony No. 40 K550, and Symphony No. 41 K551. These were the last important orchestral pieces he composed.

Although the symphonies were some of the best music he had written, the Viennese public were not as interested in Mozart as they had been. He was still popular outside Vienna, however, so in 1789 he set out to see what opportunities lay elsewhere. He visited Prague, Dresden, Leipzig, and Berlin, but unfortunately returned to Vienna without the job he was looking for.

January 1790

Mozart's *Così fan Tutte* ("Women Are Like That") premieres in Vienna.

February 1790

Emperor Joseph II dies. He is succeeded by his brother, who becomes Emperor Leopold II.

Back in Vienna, Mozart devoted his time mainly to writing opera. The librettist of *Don Giovanni*, Lorenzo Da Ponte, provided an opera called *Così fan Tutte* ("Women Are Like That"); Pietro Metastasio and Caterino Mazzolà wrote *La Clemenza di Tito* ("The Clemency of Titus"); and Emanuel Schikaneder wrote the libretto for *Die Zauberflöte* ("The Magic Flute").

When these operas were first performed in 1790 and 1791, they restored Mozart's reputation, but he found the extra work tiring and was often ill. Constanze had given birth to a baby girl, Anna Maria, in 1789, but she had died on the same day. In July 1791, their sixth child, Franz Xaver Wolfgang, was born. Then Mozart was commissioned to write a requiem (a church service for a funeral). He was delighted at the chance to write more church music.

The Magic Flute

Many people think *Die Zauberflöte*, or *The Magic Flute*, is Mozart's greatest work. It tells of Prince Tamino and Papageno, who use a magic flute and bells to rescue Tamino's lover Pamina. In their adventures they meet the wicked Queen of the Night and the Moor Monostasos.

Left: The sinister Queen of the Night sings one of the best-known arias in *Die Zauberflöte*. Here she can be seen at the center of a set from a 20th-century production of the opera.

1790

Constanze goes to the spa town of Baden to treat her illness.

July 1791

The Mozarts' sixth child, Franz Xaver Wolfgang (1791–1844), is born.

Mozart's Requiem

While he was working on the requiem, Mozart became ill again. The doctors had no idea what was wrong. In November 1791, he took to his bed, but still managed to continue working. His condition grew worse, and on the morning of December 5, 1791, he died, a few weeks before his 36th birthday.

Mozart's body was taken away the next day and blessed at the Crucifix Chapel of St. Stephen's in Vienna. It was a simple funeral ceremony, attended by family and a few friends. He was then buried in the cemetery of St. Marx in an unmarked common grave. This was not

Above: The people of Prague were very fond of Mozart. This bust is in the park of the Villa Betramka, where he stayed when visiting the city.

because Mozart was poor or no longer considered a great composer, as is sometimes suggested, but because it was the custom at the time.

Constanze was left with their two surviving sons, Carl Thomas and Franz Xaver. She continued to support her husband even after his death by organizing his manuscripts and publicizing his work. She remarried in 1809. Mozart's pupil Franz Xaver Süssmayr completed the requiem, the last of a huge number of compositions by one of the greatest composers of all time.

September 1791
La Clemenza di Tito and *Die Zauberflöte* are premiered in the same month.

November 20, 1791
Mozart becomes ill, but continues working from his bed.

Over the course of his life, Mozart had written more than 40 symphonies, 27 piano concertos, more than 15 operas, a great deal of church music, and hundreds of other pieces. More important than the number of compositions is the beauty of the music he wrote. His music was enjoyed, played, and studied during his lifetime, but also long after. While many composers of his time have been forgotten, Mozart's music lives on. His operas, symphonies, concertos, and church music such as the requiem are performed regularly today, more than 200 years after his death, and copies of his music are still being sold. Few other composers have left such a legacy of wonderful music.

Below: Mozart's music is still a popular choice for concerts. Here, the violinist Anne-Sophie Mutter is playing his Violin Concerto K219 in 1996.

The poisoning myth

Some people think that Mozart's death was not from natural causes. It has been suggested that there was a curse on the requiem he was writing when he died. There is also a story that he was poisoned by a rival composer. However, the truth is not so sinister: Mozart simply died from an undiagnosed infectious illness made worse by overwork and poor health.

December 5, 1791
Wolfgang Amadeus Mozart dies. He is buried in the cemetery of St. Marx, in a suburb of Vienna.

2006
Concerts and operas are performed around the world to celebrate the 250th anniversary of Mozart's birth.

Glossary

aria (Italian for "song") a song in an opera, sung by one of the leading singers.

brass instruments the family of instruments that includes the trumpet, horn, trombone, and tuba. They are wind instruments (the player blows into them to make the sound) and are generally made of brass.

Catholic a member of the Christian church headed by the pope in Rome.

chamber music music for small groups of musicians, usually numbering between two and eight performers. These are known as a duet (or duo) for two, trio for three, quartet for four, quintet for five, sextet for six, septet for seven, and octet for eight performers.

choir a group of singers. Most music for the church is written for choir and organ, or choir and orchestra.

chorus a choir of singers in an opera. The pieces they sing in the opera are also known as choruses.

clavichord a small keyboard instrument with a very soft sound. It is too quiet to be used to give concerts, but was a popular instrument in many homes before the piano became fashionable.

commission to pay for a composer to write a piece of music. Freelance composers make some of their money from music commissioned by rich patrons, opera companies, or the church.

compose to write music. A composer invents new pieces of music and writes them down using musical notes.

concerto a piece of music for a solo instrument (or sometimes more than one solo instrument) and orchestra. Many concertos have sections in which the soloist can show off how brilliantly or movingly he or she can play.

conductor the person who directs an orchestra. The conductor uses a small stick, known as a baton, to beat time and make sure the orchestra plays the music at the right speed.

court the palace of a nobleman, or the people who lived and worked in one. In 18th-century Europe, each region's rulers lived in a court.

dedicate to write a piece of music in someone's honor. In pieces that have been commissioned, composers often write a dedication, a tribute to say thank you, to the person who has paid for the music.

freelance working for oneself rather than for an employer in a regular job. Freelance musicians make their money by writing music, playing in concerts, or giving lessons.

harpsichord a keyboard instrument that makes its sound by plucking strings. It has a bright, tinkling sound.

Holy Roman Empire a group of European Catholic states with their own princely rulers, headed by the Austrian emperor. The empire stretched over much of central Europe until the 19th century.

improvise to make up music as you are playing or singing, rather than playing from music written down on paper.

keyboard instruments a family of instruments played by pressing keys.

libretto (Italian for "little book") the words written for a composer to set to music as an opera.

Mass the Catholic service of prayers and the blessing of bread and wine, representing the body and blood of Christ. The words of the service are often set to music by composers.

movement a section of a symphony, concerto, or sonata.

opera a drama in which the words are sung rather than spoken.

orchestra a large group of musicians. Instruments usually include members of the string, woodwind, brass, and percussion families.

organ a large keyboard instrument that makes its sound by pumping air through special pipes. Organs are usually found in churches, but there are also "chamber" organs for smaller concert halls.

patron a person who pays for a work of art, for example by commissioning a piece of music. The system where a nobleman, or wealthy person, employs musicians to play and write music is known as patronage.

percussion instruments a family of instruments that make a sound when hit with sticks or banged together. The family includes drums and metal instruments such as the cymbals and the triangle.

piano a keyboard instrument that makes its sound by hitting strings with small wooden hammers covered with felt, unlike the earlier harpsichord, in which the strings are plucked.

premiere the first performance of a piece of music, a play, etc.

prodigy a person, particularly a child, who has an outstanding talent for something, such as playing a musical instrument. Mozart was considered a child prodigy.

quartet a group of four musicians, or a piece of music for four musicians. The most common combination is the string quartet, which is made up of two violins, a viola, and a cello.

republic a country governed by the people or their elected representatives, rather than by an emperor or monarch.

requiem a piece of church music for a funeral. The requiem is a setting of the Latin words of the Catholic Mass for the dead, and is sung by a choir, often with an orchestra.

solo a piece of music for one player or singer. The person who plays a solo is called a soloist.

sonata a piece of music for a keyboard, such as the piano, or a solo instrument accompanied by a keyboard. Sonatas are usually in two to four movements.

stringed instruments a family of instruments including the violin, viola, cello, and double bass. The strings can be plucked with the fingers, but are usually played with a bow made of wood and horse-hair pulled across the strings.

symphony a piece of music for an orchestra, usually in several sections called movements.

woodwind instruments a family of wind instruments which includes the flute, oboe, clarinet, and bassoon. They were originally made of wood, but today are made using metal or plastics instead.

Bibliography

Amadeus, a film based on the play by Peter Shaffer, dir. Milos Forman, 1984

The Cambridge Mozart Encyclopedia, ed. Cliff Eisen and Simon P. Keefe, Cambridge University Press, 2006

The Cambridge Music Guide, ed. Stanley Sadie and Alison Latham, published by Cambridge University Press, 1985

The Chronicle of Classical Music, by Alan Kendall, published by Thames & Hudson, 1994

The Faber Pocket Guide to Mozart, by Nicholas Kenyon, published by Faber & Faber, 2005

Mozart (The Master Musicians series), by Julian Rushton, published by Oxford University Press, 2006

Mozart: An Extraordinary Life, by Julian Rushton, published by Associated Board of the Royal Schools of Music, 2005

The Mozart Compendium: A Guide to Mozart's Life and Music, ed. H.C. Robbins Landon, published by Thames & Hudson, 1996

Mozart's Women, by Jane Glover, published by Macmillan, 2005

The New Grove Dictionary of Music and Musicians, ed. Stanley Sadie, published by Macmillan, 2001

The Oxford Dictionary of Opera, by John Warrack and Ewan West, published by Oxford University Press, 1992

Source for quote:

p. 43 *The New Grove Dictionary of Music and Musicians,* 2001

Some Web sites that will help you to explore Mozart's world:

www.bbc.co.uk/music/profiles/mozart.shtml
www.mozarteum.at
www.mozartproject.org

Index

Acknowledgments

Source: AA = The Art Archive.

B = bottom, C= center, L = left, R = right, T = top.

Front cover (Mozart) Alfredo Dagli Orti/The Art Archive/Corbis; (sheet music) Bettmann/Corbis; **1** © Lebrecht Music & Arts; **3** AA/Mozarteum, Salzburg; **4T** AA/Mozarteum, Salzburg/Dagli Orti; **4B** AA/ Museo Bibliografico Musicale, Bologna/Dagli Orti; **5T** The Bridgeman Art Library/Gesellschaft der Musikfreunde, Wien, Austria; **5B** AA/Mozarteum, Salzburg; **4–5** © Lebrecht Music & Arts; **7** AA/ Mozarteum, Salzburg/Dagli Orti; **6–7** © Lebrecht Music & Arts; **8** AA/Mozarteum, Salzburg; **9, 10, 11** akg-images; **13** © Lebrecht Music & Arts; **14** AA/Bibliothèque des Arts Décoratifs, Paris/Dagli Orti; **15BC** AA/Mozarteum, Salzburg/Dagli Orti; **15BR** © Photo Scala, Florence; **16** akg-images; **17T** AA/Musée du Château de Versailles/Dagli Orti; **17B, 19** akg-images; **21** AA/Museo Bibliografico Musicale, Bologna/ Dagli Orti; **20–21** © Lebrecht Music & Arts; **23** akg-images; **24** © Graham Salter/Lebrecht; **25** The Bridgeman Art Library/Private Collection; **26L** © Royal Academy of Music Coll, photograph by Clarissa Bruce/Lebrecht; **26R** © Graham Salter/Lebrecht; **27T** © Lebrecht Music & Arts; **27B** © Stiftung Mozart/ John Van Hasselt/Corbis; **26–27** © Lebrecht Music & Arts; **28** The Bridgeman Art Library/Musée de la Ville de Paris/Musée Carnavalet, Paris; **29, 30** AA/Mozarteum, Salzburg/Dagli Orti; **33** The Bridgeman Art Library/Gesellschaft der Musikfreunde, Wien, Austria; **32–33** © Lebrecht Music & Arts; **34** The Bridgeman Art Library/Private Collection; **35, 36** akg-images; **37** AA/National Museum, Budapest/Dagli Orti; **38** AA/ Mozarteum, Salzburg/Dagli Orti; **39** akg-images; **40TR** akg-images/Erich Lessing; **40CL** © Bettmann/ Corbis; **41T** akg-images; **41B** © 2003, Photo Scala, Florence/Fotografica Foglia; **42** akg-images; **43** AA/ Musée Carnavalet, Paris/Dagli Orti; **44** akg-images/Erich Lessing; **45** AA/Museum der Stadt Wien/Dagli Orti; **46** © 2003, Photo Scala, Florence/HIP; **47** akg-images/Erich Lessing; **49** AA/Mozarteum, Salzburg; **48–49** © Lebrecht Music & Arts; **50** AA/Mozart Museum, Villa Bertramka, Prague/Dagli Orti; **51** AA/ Burcardo Theatre coll/Dagli Orti; **52** © Lebrecht Music & Arts; **53** AA, Mozart Apartment, Vienna/Dagli Orti; **54C** © BPL/Lebrecht; **54–55** AA/Museo Teatrale alla Scala, Milan/Dagli Orti; **55TL** akg-images/by permission of P.H.Sand; **55TR** akg-images; **56** © Lebrecht Music & Arts; **57** AA/Mozarteum, Salzburg/ Dagli Orti; **58** akg-images/Gérard Degeorge; **59** © Robin Del Mar/Lebrecht.